Zen Elegies

ANDREI BRONNIKOV

Zen Elegies

REFLECTIONS

Copyright ©2010 Andrei Bronnikov

Published by Reflections

All rights reserved. No part of this publication may be reproduced or transmitted in any form or by any means, electronic or mechanical, including photocopy, recording, or any information storage and retrieval system, without permission in writing from the publisher.

Printed in the United States of America

Zen Elegies
by Andrei Bronnikov

ISBN: 978-90-79625-03-1

Zen Elegies

I

A gray sky. Waves pound the cliff. A lonely bird is up there.
    What else do you need to be happy?
Between two languages, like Tiresias, with no words and almost
    no feelings,
You weigh your loneliness on scales of the emaciated heart.
Look, you aren't the first one or the last one, who is into it,
But you do believe that you are that one who can tell us about it.
Speak, if you can, if the noise of the wind is not driving you crazy.
Speak, if the mad cry of a seagull won't tell us much more.
Speak, if your heart or anything else inside you would not let
    you down —
Since how much is left for you the Sirens on the rocks do not know,
Neither the god from the ancient books nor this grass;
Nobody does. Nature isn't inclined to think or to know.
She simply stands there as a painting on easel
While someone's observing the landscape, you, me, all our rush,
Observing all this with a mindless look of a baby
By the sea that is washing away our castles of sand
So definitely and forever.

II

Forget all your misery; after all, you come here to experience at
    least something.
There was nothing like this where you came from; there was no joy
    and no pain.
Only here where your consciousness is becoming alive inside your
    blood in the depths of your veins —
Only here you can see everything as it *is*.
All new cities are similar to the ones that you've seen before;
There is the same twinkle in the eyes of your lover and you
    recognize it,
Though you don't remember where you've seen all this.
You just say: this is mine, and that is not mine.
Your soul is squeezed between heavy stones like a sarcophagus in
    the Egyptian temple.
Your soul senses the gravity of the world — all these countless atoms,
All these mysterious fields and influences — all are pushing on you
    and leaving their traces.
By accumulating all the imprints, step by step, you become
    a replica of this world.
Now, anywhere you go, all will see with whom and where you have
    been, and who you've become.
When you arrived, your soul was like a parchment scroll with
    ancient scripts —
A fragile and thin scroll with mysterious signs and images of
    magical beasts.
When you will have to depart, all this will turn into a landscape;
    wrinkles and voids will appear.
Mountain passes, rivers, woods, cities, islands — everything what
    you have seen will come true.
Everything will materialize; everything will be raised from the

letters and signs.
Hieroglyphs will turn into roads and their intersections, birds will turn into lovers.
Everything will come to life and find its meaning.
The brittle scroll will become elastic, flexible, damp.
Plants and animals will run in the valleys and higher, in the mountains; there will be people there as well.
Only you won't be there.
You'll disappear forever, having given your blood and your flesh to the world.
All that was said in those scripts would come true and be incarnated,
But you would not see it.

III

Fate, sing to us your morose songs, until the day is gone.
Swimmer in the dark sea, man with no hope, your time is short,
    but you don't know it.
You take into yourself more and more, as if you could contain it all.
These creatures look at you innocently, but their instructions are simple;
They reach you at your top and put you mercilessly down,
And you can't resist, being blinded by their pureness.
This luminous skin hides what you are looking for. Try to penetrate
    into it.
It's absolutely not what you thought; they are full of mystery because
    death is behind them.
Look at their palms — everything is told there, but you can see
    even more in their fingers.
Autumn, rains are on your streets, winds blow over the roofs,
    avenues are deserted.
It is the best time to love, expecting no answer.
Animals are too clever to think of us; they are busy with their own things.
Take the hand of your lover while she allows you to do so;
    she doesn't know what it is.
Gods of empty sidewalks. Outcast angels. They are crowding here
    like clouds upon a river.
Ask them what it is that she wants.

IV

After visiting those somber places, I have found myself in a desert.
Many people were there and they all had something to tell.
Sometimes it seemed to me that they spoke the same things, only started at different times,
Therefore their choir sounded so discordant.
They absolutely did not know why they were there, but they believed that they knew.
Sounds, colors, smells, and anything else — all was excessive.
There was so much of everything there (it was multiplied many times by itself)
That all small, hardly sensible, hidden things have vanished
While all big ones have grown even bigger to become awkwardly great, inappropriate and unneeded.
There was no middle way, no kindness; there was no shoulder to lean the head on.
It was a meaningless world.

V

I've lived such a long life that I don't even know why I have started
    all this.
I've been to places where they don't shake hands with girls,
But the girls give looks that penetrate straight into the heart.
In those places, the moon doesn't shine above cities,
    preferring the fields in the suburbs,
And dry grasses give up all hopes to the sky, and snows cover all
    songs of the earth.
There I saw dead people, who didn't know that they were the dead,
And I saw living people who were alive.
Once I lived among them, fell in love and expected an answer.
I was able to see the meaning in each turn of the road and hear it
    in the sound of each subway train.
I met every new day with a secret hope that it would be the first one.
I don't know why I never thought of using the entire measure of my
    love
To be buried under it like an ancient prince under his
    heavy tombstone.

VI

Don't be afraid, my friend,
This is just life.
And this is the best way to learn about time.
The mechanical clock is a toy, an illusion.
Time is measured only by the number of moments you *are* alive;
And there is no other reason to live at all.
Unlike animals, we are able to mind time,
And therefore we are somehow involved in the production of time.
Our existence makes time possible because if we were not there,
Then no one would know about time,
And all things would freeze in a single eternal moment.
Our existence gives the dynamics of change to the world,
Which is, perhaps, the only reason for the being of mankind.
And the reason for the personal being is to form a cell of time,
So that time won't be discontinued for any moment.
Who would possibly need this? We are unable to know,
As a tiny atom does not know its place in the universe.
Even so, it's improbable that all this is just a laboratory of some superb creatures.
Most likely it is something else. Something we almost can't think of.
Maybe what we call "time" is an object like this mountain or that castle.
Or maybe it is a set of colored glasses in gods' kaleidoscope;
Or flowers scattered in the field; every flower is somebody's fate.
A flower. It is picked up and somebody's time is ended.
But even then, something still can be done —
It can stand for a while in a vase on a table
Where someone adores its fading freshness

And then go down to where won't be any time,
But where its tender roots are silently growing
To become a new flower and start it all over.

VII

Hurry up, hurry up, as this thin shell is still holding what soon will
 break free.
Hurry up, hurry up, as you still do not know that all your myths
 are just myths.
You have time between this and that, and you have to make choices.
Possession and possibility are behind you; losses and a new search
 lie ahead.
Here — between Scylla and Charybdis of your feelings — your heart
 is beating like a fish in the brothers' hands.
And yet there is hope — this wormwood-like bitterness of life.
Only here, at the threshold of pain, only here anything still can happen.
And this is unstoppable. This is written in the books where
 everything has been accounted for until the very last second.
Where's your place? What do you have to do in order to save just
 a single moment?
You who turn water into wine, can you control a simple flight table?
Can you alter the entire course of the universe to turn it onto your
 own orbits?
Everything has been predicted by the ancients;
Everything, including the departure and arrival times, including
 time to check in and receive the luggage.
Where is a place for at least one of your dark and deep feelings?
They are flying above, not touching anything here.
They are the reflections. But there is no reality either —
 they are the reflections of other reflections.
While you were waiting for her, the earth had moved one million
 miles away.
Now we are in a different place.
The earth is against us — it was always dusty and hard.

The stars are against us — each shot of them hit straight into your heart.
The stars are revived myths. Look, there are so many of them in this book!
But you are alone and you don't know where the exit is.
You who speak to the gods, you don't know how to talk to her.
You have no words left; all your words have been used like disposable dishes.
You'd better keep silently going on your own way out there —
Above empty lands, above black dazzling skies, in the heights.

VIII

Poets feeding babies with own blood. Games with gods. Ancient
    passions of flesh.
Remember this day, since it may turn to be the last one so easily.
Where were you when they gave out their things? How many hands
    did you hold in your hands?
How many hands did touch upon you? What did you do when they
    all were going away?
It is empty and silent up here (only turbines are making noise).
Maybe gods are just molecular structures?
Now we know much more. But can we hear a Siren? Can we see
    a goddess rising from foam?
Who is trying to deafen the ears? Who is afraid of a glimpse,
    being unable to stand the truth of reality?
Why had you crucified yourself, god of Abraham? What is the
    meaning of sacrifice — love or pain?
Esoteric buses carry pilgrims. Sinai is in smoke again, as if it's
    expecting another flood.
Where is that one who can understand all your pain when you're
    being crucified and they roar with laughter, shouting
"C'mon, brother, c'mon, build your temple! It's going to be good for us.
You have done a great job so far; we all like it.
Well, maybe too much blood and the bones protrude from the skin,
But by and large it's okay; we all are very much,
    very much satisfied"?

IX

But all this pain, all this burden of loss — why?
The inability to speak and the inability to be silent — why?
Who has made it so that the giver doesn't take, and the taker
    isn't able to give?
Where is the middle path that you keep searching for?
Your life has began not yesterday, and you have already seen
    a number of houses and streets.
You have said many times "hello" and a few times "good bye".
You have seen many people, but even more of those fleshless
    shining angels —
They gathered there on the large screens around you.
You couldn't touch them. How many people do you really know?
Like Thomas, how many times were you able to make sure that they
    all were indeed in the flesh?
But even then, after they've gone, did you see any of them again?
Your brain is overloaded with information, and you don't know
    what to do about it.
All these shapeless flows have no color, no smell —
It would be enough for you just a little bit, but they keep coming
    and coming.
Does it make any sense if nobody hears you?
You speak to yourself, even when you are standing before them.
All the words which you say are the words that they know,
Otherwise communication would be impossible.
Smooth black fishes of thoughts, depths of the heart, where the hot
    blood is flowing —
Your shell covers all this, leaving at the surface only the
    meaningless words.
They all know where to look and what to listen to,
But this doesn't make it easier for you.
You are fastened with the nails of your fate to the planks of this world,

Your arms are stretched as if for hugs, but no one's going in there;
You feel so much pain. But nowhere to go, until a boy from
    the third row
Gives you a pint of vinegar in his childish helmet,
And you breathe it in with a sigh of relief
To disappear forever.

X

Like that ancient king who returned to his island
All days long you hope for a miracle,
As if there were no places where you could be as you used to be.
Alien cities are in your eyes and a foreign language is
    heard everywhere.
Who are these people that have possessed your heart?
Who are these gods that have driven you into this situation?
No reply. Nature does not know a means to ease your pain.
But you can do it yourself.
See, all is not that bad.
At least, you can make choices now.
You can move, not knowing where you will arrive —
For all what you see is not a guarantee that it is what it is;
And all what you know is too small to be loved,
But it does something to you
And after some time you won't recognize yourself.
Kill the pity for yourself and the others —
Here is the sword with which you cut off the pain.
Kill everything that is not needed for death.
Be prepared for it because it is coming.
It will take you to where you have never been,
You can't drag with you there your mind, love, feelings, money,
Except maybe some coins to pay for the ferry,
Though they'll probably allow someone like you for free.
You'd better stay with us for a while —
Look and see that you don't need tears.
Everything is so unreliable here. One poor instant
    which is lighted up in the dark by an invisible someone.
One moment of loneliness on the seashore

While a ship is sailing away from you, getting smaller and smaller,
Leaving you here all alone with your sorrow.

FEBRUARY–AUGUST 2005

Towards The Incredibly Small Ones

I

I am on my way towards the incredibly small ones.
Like some new buddha, I am illuminated by the meaninglessness of
 all that surrounds me.
The singer with no song. The poet with no rhyme and no goal. The
 one who has rejected everything.
I've lived such a long life that I don't even know why I have started
 all this.
So often I was in despair because it seemed to me that I wasn't
 understood by anyone.
Perhaps, it wasn't easy for them to understand me when I stood
 before them silently.
They probably thought that they knew all my thoughts,
And that my thoughts were the same as their own.
They couldn't grasp me as a whole, but didn't see the small details either.
Such people are called "blind", and I lived among them.
When I let them read my writings, they always said to me
 "it looks like that" or "it is like this".
Some pointed out mistakes, expecting me to improve things that
 were there.
The most of them, however, were silent, not noticing their presence
 in my world at all.
It seemed to them that everything was just the same, for once and
 forever.
And they laughed at me. They did not believe me when I told them
That a single line could change the fragile balance of the world,
And a single new song could create two or even three universes.
People who didn't believe me were all around me.
I lived among them and, gradually, I got used to my pain.

II

I look at this world with impassivity that amazes me.
Seeing an ugly person I admit ugliness.
Seeing a beauty I think: "oh how beautiful she is" and I'm not
    flattering.
I see things how they are, but I have no words for them. We don't
    have too many words.
How do we call that feeling which we get after have perceived
    anything deeply?
We have our good feelings, and we have anger and bitterness,
    but all these feelings are not enough.
These are simple concepts, and their combinations cannot be one
    whole thing.
I have no words that have not been used by anyone else ever before.
Perhaps, what I have are very small sensations, short flashes,
The prototypes of reality which is not damaged by thousands of
    contexts.
How can one capture these proto feelings — these small displacements?
Their weight is comparable to the weight of sunlight spots on
    the wall;
Their order is unknown and given to us in the complex terms that
    we are unable to comprehend.

III

There is not much light in these houses, and everything that was
    here has been taken away long ago.
What has been left behind is: a chair, a table, a sofa, a curtain with
    the sunlight on it, and a wonderful city behind the
    wide-open window.
There are so many people out there on the streets, going somewhere
    in pairs,
Sometimes in triples, or even as an entire group.
All of them seem to have a certain focus — a point of the perspective
    to go to.
Who gave them this pulse, or maybe they move chaotically,
    having no target, no goal?
Making an appointment, they do not know what it is, and they can't
    understand its meaning;
There is a paper that tells them: do this and do that — a technical
    manual of their lives.
Unwritten laws are reflected in the windscreens of their cars;
    somehow they all know where they're going.
But there is one beautiful lady in this city, who doesn't want
    to follow them all.
She sits by the window and looks at the sky, white on blue.
She waits for a telephone call, and when the doorbell rings,
    she won't open.
She enjoys her sweet presentiments. Her hand is on her belly.
The skin is so soft down there.

IV

We are overwhelmed by the idea of vision. All we do is see,
    even when talking and listening.
These transparent tentacles entangle our world, giving us no
    chance to discover reality.
I would like to think of something, but I instantly see the object,
    which, indeed, makes no sense.
How would it be to not see or hear or sense? What would we do
    then?
Perhaps, we would stand like temples with the images of gods who
    can't see themselves.
Gods must be blind; otherwise they would constantly suffer from
    the need to re-size the picture,
For no one can see the incredibly small ones without losing the big
    ones from sight.

V

Once, when I was a boy, I carved a model ship from a piece of
 wood and had cut the palm of my hand.
It was bleeding fast. I was surprised, but not frightened.
And I asked myself: if I lost all my blood, then who would be able
 to return it to me?
They placed cotton wool on my wound and it became red.
I still have a scar on my palm.

VI

Why do we search for the beloved one where she can't be found?
It's not easy; we start with a look, which is directed inside.
Then we speak; always speak out a certain word.
Imagine love of a dumb and deaf man who only had vision and
    senses of skin.
But if he were a blind man wearing gloves, then how could
    he fall in love?
Love is a visual, geometrical concept — the ancients knew this.
There is some figure whose curves are pleasant for eyes.
Usually it is due to the place in the space where the body is,
And the place where it moves to (even standing still, it moves
    with the waves).
The latter occurs because of breathing the air in and out,
    since we all need oxygen here.
Therefore, even when lovers are silent, they know each other with
    their breaths.
Coincidence of waves (i.e., all figures of the body) throughout
    their extent — this is what love is.
But is this indeed what we search for?

VII

The memory gives us a strange feeling that all this already was.
The memory can't remember itself and always asks us for help.
When we need it, we call it to us, as if it were a dog that we spoil with treats.
It serves us; it does it so well.
Sometimes it shows character, not letting us forget things that we don't want to remember.
Then we name it "consciousness" and let it go away, throwing a ball or a stick.
Where is all this happening?
Which measure do we use to measure these spaces?
I have been to the places where paintings are kept.
Usually a painting has the form of a square or a rectangle, rarely — a circle or an ellipse.
I have listened to what is called "music" (the imitation of loving as breathing with moving the air).
I have observed the constructions of mind in the theater and architecture (the imitation of loving as a geometry).
I have tried to sing my own song, being out of breath because of my feelings and thoroughly analyzing the intervals of sound.
People didn't understand me, believing it was just a joke.
People always intend to search for a meaning, which makes them different from animals.
I'd better sing my songs to cows and birds.
For there is no other meaning except that one which is given in breathing, in the wave of the surrounding world.
I'm sighing when I'm poignant. I'm out of breath when having

   pain or pleasure —
This is the only song that was given to me by heaven.

VIII

We've left home and would hardly be back.
Some have something like a lamp or a couch with them, sometimes other things too.
It seems to them that everything is just like it was, and they have never left this place.
They are running from death, renewing their houses, and buying more things
While death looks at them kindly, like a country dog.
It has been with us for a while.
The most fearless ones live as if there were no death, as if that dog was not sitting out there.
In a way, they are right, since nothing has much meaning,
And it is better to throw a bone to the dog than listen to a growl.
On the day when you came to understand how the skies were moving, you thought that you had become eternal, like a pyramid.
You managed to comprehend all the mechanics of stars, all their orbits and parallaxes.
You were so happy that day, and the next day, and the day after.
You were waiting for a reward because you had brought to the master all he wanted.
You believed you had rights to ask for better love and a warmer place.
But when all of this has come true, you've thought that they cheated you again —
Maybe you wanted something completely different?

IX

Ivy climbs over old stones. Cliffs peacefully face the sea.
It is quiet. Come into this world, as into your own home (no one will offend you here).
You will be calmly observing things, giving them no meaning.
You will not be in hurry anymore. You will not be suffering from the absence of any meaning.

X

All the doors are open for you at the top of the day.
The sun shines in dry grasses and burns the ground.
You have been here many times, but haven't seen anything.
Your world was filled with gray clouds of old resentments
    and illusions.
You always found fault, looking for anyone or anything to blame
    for your failures.
In such a state, you couldn't become a part of nature
Because she doesn't know resentments, and kills and loves
    with ease.
Isn't it the indifference you were searching for? It was hard
    to achieve.
Your heart became a stone of tears when your pain came back to
    you.
That was hard, and you thought: "I can't bear all this anymore".
Imagine if mountains could feel the weight of all their stones —
Then so much screaming and pain would surround us. But this does
    not happen.
Someone has deprived nature of feelings, having left behind
    the sun in the grass,
The bumblebees that are swarming here and there,
The little ants on the rocks.
And then, even smaller, some dust, smaller and smaller —
Something else out there, but still

the same happy indifference
Of the incredibly small ones.

FEBRUARY–AUGUST 2005

At The Borders Of Light

I

Breaking through to the light. It's not easy, but we
Keep going, conquering the pieces of space,
Invisible cubes in the geometry of the world.
Growing one from the other, filling in what still
Remains empty, no matter how much we would grow
Into it, no matter how long our sprouts would be.
It remains empty and free for the coming shoots.
Day is waiting for us and, making our run,
We break another frontier, and know no limits.

II

Circles. For others. You know the pain of return.
Leaving, we never come back. You stay where you are.
It only seems to you that you're making a step. Dying,
You grow into other being while they find the replacement
For you; they easily find the replacement at the place where
Once you were loved. This is a circle. Life substitutes you with
Something else. And after the replacement has taken place
Life is again full of joy like a widow who has found
Another husband. We are going on the tangent to the circle
With no intersection to the place where you are.
Our worlds are different. Crossing this point, we cannot
Become anything bigger in the circles of your life.
But our line is longer than any circle. It stretches from
Anywhere to nowhere. Only here, in this point
You can notice slight motion: we are passing by.
Always passing by. Night on your streets. Light is
Balancing between this and that, making you believe
That you are still here. Being reflected from objects,
Light makes you see things as you see them.
We remain at the other side of all this,
At the other side of the world.

III

And no matter how persistent you stare, your pupil would not
Discern anything in the dark beyond the borders of light
Where light ends and not the darkness but the other
Space starts, the space of the other light. And this has no end.
Overlapping, these spaces cover the surfaces of the world.
One inside the other, and so on, and so forth. Your existence
Remains closed at one of the borders, which is not bad if you
Know that the motion on the circle is eternal. You leave
To come back when they replace you with something similar.
That is why they are disappointed by you. They've had time
To get used to one thing, but now they have to get used to
    the other.
Only the motion along the line can save you from
The constant return. It is like death. Because if you
Move along the line, you leave for certain. Like a spacecraft
Which leaves the orbit of Earth. No matter what speed.
Even at low speed you overcome gravitation and leave.
Fear does hold you. This is stronger than gravitation,
Rather, it is your gravitation. The power that is able to hold
Not only you but the planets on the circles of life.
Certain, reliable power. There is one way out of here —
To leave, to get out of the limits of this world, breaking
    through to the outside.
This is what we are doing. Growing into
Invisible. Every day slowly growing into invisible.
And this is the way. This is how light goes away.
There, in the lamp, there is a hot fire, but at the distance
It is getting colder. The rays go away and they go forever;
There is no limit for light. If there was no wall and no
Other obstacle, then light from your lamp would go forever.

So do we. Further and further from the initial flame, from the
Fire that has given our birth. We are in the emptiness of the
>   world.
The rays. Subjugating the space, its pieces, those invisible
Cubes in the geometry of the world. Leaving, scattering, we
>   lose each other.
The rays become split.

IV

And only the darkness into which the ray hits remains the reality.
A ray: particles ordered one after another.
And someone needs to be the first one, and someone has to follow.
What does happen to the first one? Invisible to those who only follow
He runs into the dark ahead. What is the meaning of motion?
This experience is unique. When you leave you cannot leave it entirely.
But we can. Leaving behind this space absolutely empty.
Stripped from us, it becomes full with those who are following us.
And this has no end. Only there, at the border,
There is no one and this is the place where you cannot see
Anything of what you have had, anything of what you got used to on
    your circles.
These are your choices: to run on the circle in the comfort of habit, or
Leave. And if you leave, you never come back.
Because having left this place you won't be able to circle.
You would go up until the end, until the very last border.
And there, having looked behind, you would see a weak reflection,
    almost invisible ray of light —
These are those who are following you. This is what holding you,
Your chance to measure your way and understand that it is not a circle.
Conquering the pieces of space, invisible cubes in the geometry of
The world, we are growing one from the other, keeping doing
    our work.

In A Thundering Tube

M.

On a runaway summer, at the outskirts of the world,
through the city full of cafes, people, books and
bookstores, seamen, flowers, girls on bikes, the Chinese,
channels, etc., we will go and arrive to the water, a ferry,
and while the shore is drifting away and seagulls
are gliding above, and swans by the old pier,
and gray waves, and cranes —
while all this is here with us, we are hugging near
a rusty side and the day smiles at us, saying:
look, it's another flash full of life, and it's so much of this,
and up there, almost out of sight, a small plane is rushing away
across infinite skies.

I

In a thundering tube, amid shadows, we have to shout to hear each other.

II

Inclining, your face makes a weird angle with
this place in the universe.

III

The hot air and the twists of the tube going down.

IV

The immense world is hanging above us.
The book of my poems in the hands of a boy standing
near a metallic bar.

V

There is so much reality here that it becomes really scary.

VI

In the fake city that was built in a hurry,
in a mix of styles you do not have any rights;
awakening, you want to go back to sleep
to not see this low sky and this flat constructivism
which was turned into renaissance by the upper command.

VII

Demons of childhood are tearing your soul
while you're traveling through the land of
the dead like an Egyptian priest,
between the alive and the shadows,
having no power to understand who is who,
having no power to close your eyes for a second
to jump out of these orbits, out of this world.
Osiris is ruling here again, and the city
becomes the New Kingdom, and we are
celebrating the dead and the river, going out
of the banks, is covering all, penetrating into
our pores, taking us far away from here.

VIII

ὁδὸς ἄνω κάτω μία καὶ ὡυτή
ὁδὸς ἄνω κάτω μία καὶ ὡυτή
ὁδὸς ἄνω κάτω μία καὶ ὡυτή

— a blind old man is muttering.

IX

But no one does hear. They still are unable to hear,

X

Lonely song, you are pouring into the evening as if into a vessel.

XI

Dry grasses breathe autumn air, leaning down to the ground.

XII

Who, if I cried out, would hear me here?

XIII

Who, if I kept silent, would hear my silence?

XIV

Making the leap you are moving from one side of your consciousness to the other.

XV

Your hands, your look. I've been thinking about
all this for so long.

XVI

You are standing in meditation near a huge thistle at the edge of a football field.

XVII

Purple leaves and burdocks are reminding Gauguin.

XVIII

Least of all, this place looked like a temple of our love, but it turned out to be it.

XIX

O these glorious waste grounds!

XX

You look at me in search of anything
that may be like me, but that's not right.
You compare me to someone
you knew, but that's not right.
I have gone my own way at the edge
of the sky full of wreaks of the dead stars,
over rusty lands covered by the green grasses,
on the dark streets of stone cities.
Everywhere I had seen some people,
but I remembered you and when you asked
what it was that I wanted, I had told you.

XXI

Who else could have told you this?

XXII

I would like to lay down with you and forget all my pain
in a stream of compassion and warmness,
where there were no words, where you were with me,
and we're mixing our breaths, interlocking our bodies,
and yours was entwining with mine, as a snake twines
around an apple tree.

XXIII

And the sky was hanging above like a dark-blue abyss.

XXIV

The dark forest encircled children leaving the meadow;
the trees hide Adam and Eve from the jealous gods who knew
that we were like gods and this place was our temple with this
thistle and this lawn on which rabbits were slowly eating up
the leftovers of somebody's lunch and the buildings of glass
and concrete were surrounding us.

XXV

And only the thunder of the tube reminds us that we are still here.
And only the word does mean something, but is almost unheard.

XXVI

This is the way from the past into the future through the hum of the present that, in fact, is the future.

XXVII

In a thundering tube, in the moment of eternity
we are observing the essence of the world.

XXVIII

In the end, we get rid of illusions and begin seeing clearly.

XXIX

Σίβυλλα δὲ μαινομένῳ στόματι ἀγέλαστα καὶ ἀκαλλώπιστα
καὶ ἀμύριστα φθεγγομένη χιλίων ἐτῶν ἐξικνεῖται
τῇ φωνῇ διὰ τὸν θεόν

CONTENTS

Zen Elegies 7

Towards
The Incredibly
Small Ones 27

At The Borders Of Light 47

In A Thundering Tube 57

Books by Andrei Bronnikov

ROOTS OF TIME (2008)

SPECIES EVANESCENS (2009)

ZEN ELEGIES   (2009)

www.ingramcontent.com/pod-product-compliance
Lightning Source LLC
Chambersburg PA
CBHW051707040426
42446CB00008B/763